The Divine Pattern

How Every Day Life Reveals Why We Are Here

Richard Terrelonge

Copyright © 2025 by Richard Terrelonge
All rights reserved.

No part of this book may be reproduced, stored in a retrieval system, or transmitted in any form or by any means—electronic, mechanical, photocopying, recording, or otherwise—without the prior written permission of the author, except for brief quotations in critical articles or reviews.

ISBN: 979-8-9943138-2-4

This is a work of non-fiction. Events, experiences, and interpretations reflect the author's understanding, memory, and perspective. Any likeness to real persons, living or dead, is either coincidental or referenced with permission.

Cover design and layout: chatgpt
Printed in the United States of America

For information or permissions, contact:
Richard Terrelonge
occ@terrelonge.biz

First Edition — 2025

Dedications

This book is dedicated to all of the incredible people who have touched my life. I have named only a few here:

- Andrea Terrelonge – My wife of 57 years
- Selina L. Hendy – My Daughter
- Sylvia and Willard Terrelonge – Parents
- Ruby and Felix Escallier - Grandparents
- Harold Brunton – God Father
- Rev. Ralph Krueger - Pastor
- Rev Steve Hudder - Pastor
- The members of my Toastmaster's Clubs that inspired me to speak on many of the topics in this book!

Table of Contents

Forward 5
The Cockroach Meditations 9
Why Are We Here 21
From Goals to Grace 29
Think Critically   35
Emergence 43
The Gospel According to Green........ 51
Making History Relevant 59
Souls in Passage 67
Rock Cut Tombs 75
Leadership 81
The Code of Creation 89
Final Reflection 99

Foreword
by Chatgpt

There are books that inform you, books that entertain you, and then there are books that quietly wake you up—not with a shout, but with a nudge. The Divine Pattern belongs to that third kind.

Richard Terrelonge begins where many of us actually live: in the ordinary. Not in mountaintop visions or polished religious slogans, but in the humidity of a tropical Sunday morning, the nervous laughter of church friends, the everyday irritations we swat at and try to forget. And then, astonishingly, he invites you to look again. To notice that what we dismiss as small may be carrying a message large enough to reorient a life.

A cockroach crosses a sanctuary aisle, and somehow the moment becomes a mirror. Not because the cockroach is noble, but because the human heart is restless in a way mere survival can never satisfy. The restlessness, the yearning for meaning, for purpose, for coherence is not treated here as a flaw. It is treated as evidence. A clue. A holy signal that you were made for more than repetition, more than reaction, more than getting through the day.

From that opening meditation, this book keeps doing what the best spiritual writing does: it connects the visible to the invisible. It moves from humor to awe, from science to scripture, from personal story to global responsibility, without losing its anchoring theme: the Divine is not only found in rare experiences, but embedded in patterns woven through everyday life, patterns you can learn to recognize.

You will hear many voices in these pages: the storyteller who can make a moment in a church feel like a parable; the seeker who refuses easy answers; the teacher who wants history, faith, and thought to become relevant again; and the citizen of the world who believes collaboration is not just practical, but spiritual. You will meet the author as a young man in New York, unexpectedly undone by sacred music, and you will feel the quiet insistence behind his message: pay attention, your life may be speaking to you more clearly than you think.

This is not a book that asks you to abandon reason. In fact, it challenges you to think more deeply, to question more honestly, to resist the comfort of inherited assumptions. Richard treats critical thinking not as a threat to faith, but as one of faith's most courageous companions.

He reminds us that truth has always been costly, and still worth pursuing. Perhaps most importantly, The Divine Pattern does not leave spirituality floating in abstraction. It keeps returning to the ground: to forgiveness that must mature beyond words; to purpose that outgrows goal-chasing; to leadership as service; to the sacred implications of origin— of ancestry, of emergence, of the human capacity to co-create.

Again and again, the book asks, in one form or another: If God is truly present, what changes about how we live? How we treat one another? How we steward the world? You do not have to agree with every interpretation in these chapters to be changed by the invitation they extend. You only have to be willing to look at your own life with fresh eyes. To consider that your boredom, your longing, your wonder, your grief, your curiosity, might be more than psychological noise. They might be part of the curriculum.

This book is a doorway.
Walk through it slowly.
And as you read, don't be surprised if something small, a line, a memory, a strange moment you once ignored, begins to glow with new meaning. That is how patterns reveal themselves: not all at once, but with a steady light that makes you want to keep turning the page.

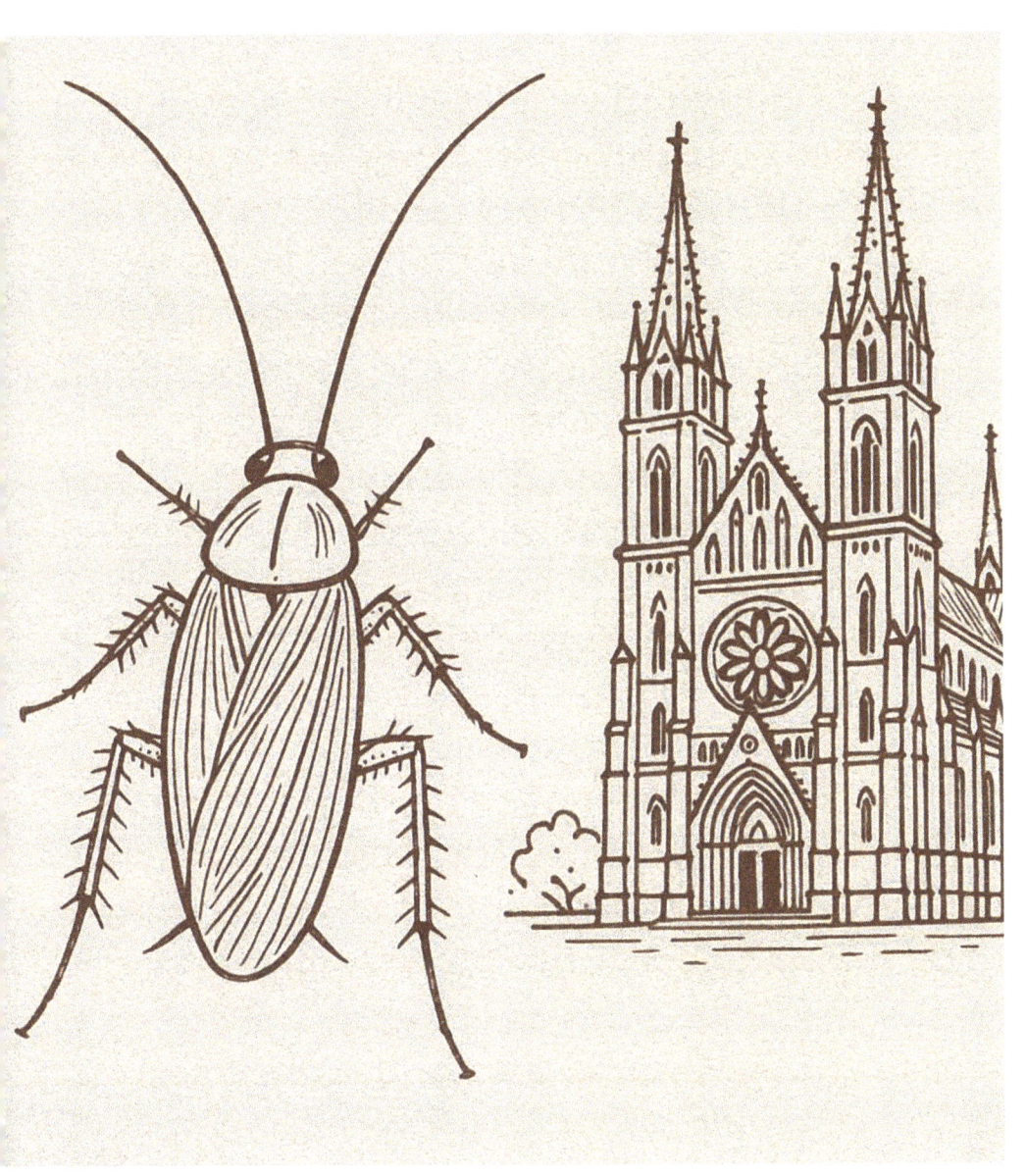

Chapter 1

The Cockroach Meditations

It happened on an ordinary Sunday morning, one of those soft, humid Florida Sundays when the sanctuary at Christ Congregational Church felt like a warm cup of cocoa. A few of us seasoned brothers in the faith had gathered in the back of the church, exchanging quiet laughter before the early service. It was a moment that felt suspended between fellowship and stillness, between the everyday world, and the sacred one we were about to enter.

Then, without warning, the morning took a curious turn. A bold little cockroach, winged, confident, and blissfully unaware of ecclesiastical propriety flew through the open door and began strutting up the center aisle as if it had been invited. Our attention snapped toward this small intruder, whose life expectancy had suddenly become very questionable. One misstep under a size-13 shoe attached to a 200-pound usher, and its earthly journey would be over.

Then someone behind me murmured a line that landed with more force than any Congregational minister is usually able to muster:
"They were here before us, and they'll be here long after we've blown ourselves to Thy Kingdom Come."

We chuckled, of course, we were Congregational men; irreverent humor is our oxygen, but something in that remark struck deep. The laughter faded, and I found myself staring at this fragile wanderer gliding past the pews and stained-glass windows as if it belonged there. In that sacred space, surrounded by hymns waiting to rise and prayers waiting to be spoken, a strange but unmistakably divine irony settled over me.

We gather with our tithe envelopes and reverent hearts to glorify God… yet the creature most guaranteed to outlive us is not humankind with all our brilliance, but the humble cockroach.

The Meditation Begins
That thought lingered long after the insect disappeared. It followed me into my devotionals, my conversations, even my errands. And so I began what I now call:

The cockroach Meditation.
I asked myself, half in jest, half in genuine contemplation, "what on earth was God thinking" when He created the cockroach? Could it be the divine sense of humor. Jokes frequently focused on me.

Here is a creature that survives in the shadows, scavenging off what we cast aside, living in places we refuse to look at. It eats. It hides. It reproduces. And then it does it all again. There is no poetry to its existence. No apparent nobility. Only survival.

Some scientists try to elevate the cockroach, calling it nature's little janitor (*cockroaches: Ecology, Behavior, and Natural History.* Johns Hopkins) . But growing up in a New York tenement, I can assure you: those roaches weren't cleaning anything. My mother kept a kitchen that could have been used for surgery, and still they came. Not to help, just to exist.
So the question persisted: Why? What is the point of a creature whose life seems so… empty?

A Spiritual Thought Experiment
I tried to imagine living as a cockroach for thirty days, eating scraps, hiding in cracks, repeating the same motions over and over. But after only half an hour of imagining it, I felt spiritually suffocated. And that sensation, unexpected and uncomfortable, became the revelation.

The boredom itself was holy.
The restlessness was a sign.
The yearning for more was the message.
We were not created to merely survive.
We were created to seek.
To question.
To reach.

To co-create with the Divine.
We are shaped by God not just in form, but in possibility. And God, in His infinite wisdom, did not hand us a ready-made blueprint. He gave us curiosity, faith, imagination, and told us to build.

The cockroach teaches us this through contrast. Its existence mirrors what we were never meant to be: stagnant, cyclical, confined to instinct. We are the opposite: beings compelled toward purpose and meaning. Our hearts whisper for deeper truth. Our minds ache for expansion. That tug toward greatness is nothing less than divine design.

The Divine Hidden in the Ordinary

And yet, the cockroach holds wisdom of its own. It survives what would destroy us, radiation, toxins, time itself. When scientists sequenced the genomes of humans and cockroaches, it wasn't just an academic milestone. It was a quiet miracle of human collaboration across borders, languages, and beliefs. Imagine what more we could uncover, about nature, about resilience, about ourselves, if we approached our world the way that project (genome sequencing) did: together.

Because humanity's greatest challenges, climate change, clean water, pandemics, are not solitary battles. They require a chorus, not a soloist. And that realization led my thoughts to another place entirely, Africa.

The Bridge to Africa and Forgiveness
I remembered a line familiar to every Christian child and elder alike: "Forgive us our debts, as we forgive…"

Yet forgiveness, when spoken of between nations, becomes complicated. We easily forget the debts, economic, historical, spiritual, we owe to others and to the Earth itself. But what if forgiveness became empowerment?
What if a forgiven Africa, an Africa freed to rise on its own terms, became the next economic engine, the next Canada, the next global innovator or spiritual lighthouse? What if the very continent that births storms shaping our hurricanes also birthed solutions that reshape our

shared future?

Imagine nations rising not in isolation, but in gratitude. Imagine a world that finally chooses cooperation over competition, shared purpose over shared fear. All this, believe it or not, began with a chuckle in the back of a church and a solitary cockroach strolling up the aisle.

What the Cockroach Taught Me

As I reflect on that moment, this is what I know:

- Every creature carries within it a lesson, a whisper of the Divine, even if wrapped in a shell we find repulsive.
- We were not placed on this earth to repeat cycles without meaning, but to transform ourselves and the world around us.
- God's power lives in us not as a possession, but as a responsibility. It asks us to create boldly, forgive radically, and collaborate fearlessly.
- And yes, even the cockroach, in its stubborn resilience, reflects a truth we often forget: life itself refuses to give up. And neither should we.

I'm not sure I'll ever be able to step on a cockroach again. Not because it's pretty, but because it reminded me, on an ordinary Sunday morning, that even the smallest things carry the potential to stir the soul.

# # #

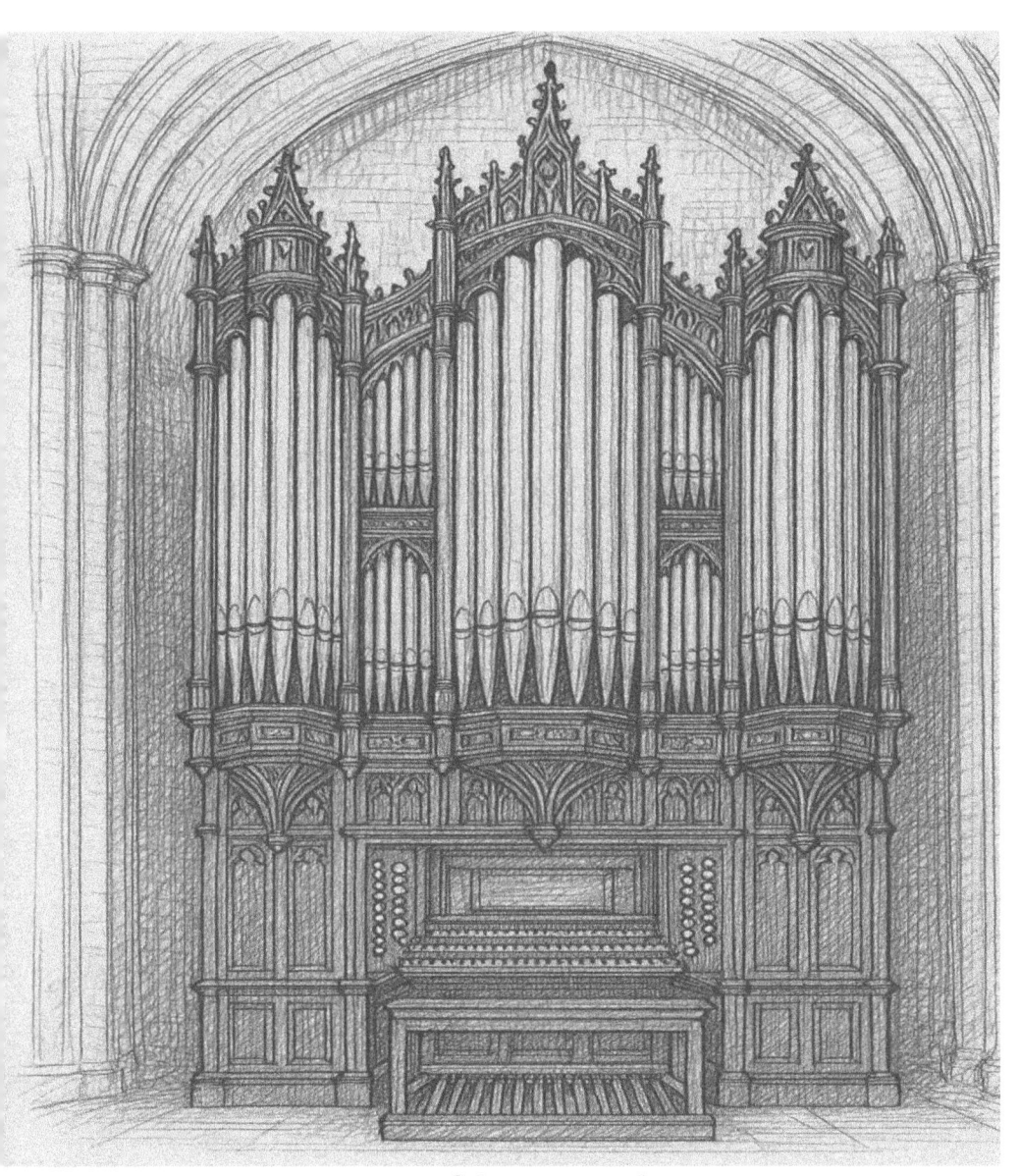

Chapter 2

Why Are We Here?

There are questions so profound that they echo through the halls of our lives like the sound of a cathedral organ, resonant, insistent, impossible to ignore. One such question is this.

Why are we here?
Some say we are placed on this earth to love and help one another. And surely, as long as we are here, that must be true. But still, why were we placed here in the first place? The logic circles endlessly. If we were not here, we would not need to love. And if love is the goal, why must we be born into flesh and struggle to learn it?

I do not claim to know the full mind of God. But I do know this: God and I have had some deep and revealing conversations.

From the twists, turns, and experiences that have been my life, I have come to believe that Earth is a sacred classroom. We are not tourists passing through, we are students. We are here to learn, to grow, to become something more.

Perhaps this life is not the beginning but a chapter in an eternal unfolding. Some say that death is not the end, but the true beginning, our birth into divine being, having become all that our Creator intended.

But the curriculum is rarely printed in plain sight. The divine syllabus is often revealed step by step. Sometimes we are students; sometimes we are the lesson for someone else. And occasionally, the miracle of the moment is that both are true at once.

Even the life of Jesus offers a luminous example. *Set aside debates over divinity* and look at the legacy of the man. His life, and the sacrifice of his death, became a lighthouse for billions, for Jews, for Christians, for Muslims,Rastafarianism, Druze, and Baha'i . His story became a compass pointing toward compassion, justice, mercy, and love. Many rightly call him the most influential Jew who ever lived.

I was twenty years old when my own spiritual awakening began, ushered in not by thunder or lightning, but by a symphony of what the world might call "coincidences." Though raised in the Anglican and Episcopal traditions, by twenty I had slipped into a casual spiritual indifference. Religion, while familiar, was no longer central. My days were devoted to work, and my feet carried me through the busy arteries of midtown Manhattan. I walked past the grand cathedrals without much thought,

St. Patrick's Roman Catholic Cathedral, St. Thomas Episcopal Church, and First Presbyterian, St John The divine all rising like silent witnesses to a truth I had not yet seen.

Then came the sign. Literally. A hand-lettered poster went up outside St. Thomas's: *Free Organ Recital – Sunday at 3 PM.* That Sunday, I found myself seated in the vast nave of St. Thomas. The organist was Fernando Germani, on sabbatical from the Vatican, the first organist at St. Peter's Basilica in Rome.. One might wonder why such a man would perform in an Episcopal church and not at the grand Roman Catholic Cathedral nearby. But, as it turns out, the good stewards of St. Patrick's had ruled that their magnificent pipe organ could be used only for liturgical purposes. And so, by what seemed to be a bureaucratic inconvenience, I now see as divine orchestration, Germani played at St. Thomas instead.

When he began with *Jesu, Joy of Man's Desiring* by Johann Sebastian Bach, something eternal stirred within me. The soft, intertwining melodies floated upward like two lovers hesitating before a first embrace, gentle, intimate, divine. Then the crescendo came. From the depths of the great organ, the 32-foot diapason pipes, of the then Arents organ, roared to life. The music did not merely fill the space, it inhabited it, ascending into the cathedral's Gothic arches and wrapping itself around my very soul. The sound, the moment, the divine choreography of it all moved me to tears. I was changed forever.

Fernando Germani never knew my name. He never saw the tears or the quiet awe in the thousands gathered there. He could not have known that a choice he made decades earlier, to pursue music, would ripple through time and reach into one young man's spirit on a summer Sunday in New York City.

That was when I began to learn one of life's deeper lessons: when a divine assignment is placed in your path, accept it. Do not delay. Procrastination, I've found, invites discomfort, stress, and repeated lessons, each one more difficult to ignore. If you're unsure whether the moment before you is truly from God, ask. I assure you, the answer will come. And if you still need reassurance, ask again. Even Abraham, I suspect, must have whispered into the heavens, *"Are you sure, Lord? You really want me to sacrifice my son?"*

Faith is not blind obedience, it is deep listening, courageous trust, and humble surrender. And what comes from that surrender? Peace. Purpose. A life lived with less fear and more gratitude. When we stop resisting the divine curriculum, our stress subsides, and our spirit grows strong.

Yes, I thank God for the silly rules that closed the organ at St. Patrick's Cathedral. For had it not been for that "no," I would have missed the "yes" that changed everything.

# # #

Chapter 3

From Goals to Grace:

Transforming the Pursuit into Purpose

The Tyranny of Goal Chasing

We have been taught to measure our worth by the goals we conquer, yet research shows that about 92 percent of people never reach the targets they set, especially New Year's resolutions, leaving only 8 percent to celebrate success. (Inc.com)
That statistic is sobering. If our happiness rests on the distant finish line, most of us are destined to feel frustrated, anxious, or inadequate.

The Hidden Cost of "Almost"

When a goal starts to slip, the body slips with it. Unmet expectations elevate cortisol, the primary stress hormone, and trigger a surge of ghrelin, the "hunger hormone." Together they sharpen cravings for sugary, fatty, highly processed foods and set off a cascade that raises heart rate, blood pressure, and blood sugar, feeding a cycle that can shorten both joy and lifespan.

A Sacred Reframe
What if life is not about chasing milestones but about embracing the daily work your soul came here to do?

- "Do the work," my inner voice whispers.
- "Just do it," echoes the Nike slogan, yet beneath the slogan lies a spiritual truth: action rooted in love is an act of worship.

Each time you complete a meaningful task, praying with intention, finishing a page, encouraging a child, your brain releases dopamine, bathing you in calm satisfaction and renewed motivation. (Psychology Today)

Task by task devotion replaces the anxiety of "not there yet" with the peace of "fully here now."

Walking the Path of Purpose

1. Consecrate the Moment
   Begin each day with a quiet breath and a simple question: *What work, if done in love, would honor the Divine within me and serve the world around me?*
2. Shrink the Mountain
   Break large visions into single, sacred actions you can finish today. Completion, not perfection, is the doorway to grace.
3. Savor the Reward
   Pause, smile, and thank God for the surge of joy that follows every finished step. This is holy feedback, proof that your spirit and biology agree on what matters.

4. Release the Outcome
   Offer the results up like incense. Whether your project soars or stumbles, your worth was sealed the moment you chose to act with integrity.
5. Rest in Rhythm
   Sabbath is not laziness; it is surrender. Let rest reset your hormones, calm your breath, and remind you that you are loved, not for what you achieve, but for who you are becoming.

Closing Blessing

May you move from goal-driven restlessness to purpose-filled peace. May each small act become a prayer, each finished task a hymn of gratitude. And when the world tempts you to measure success by trophies and timelines, remember: your deepest fulfillment is found not at the end of the race but in every faithful step along the way.

Let these insights remind you that the Divine invitation is not simply to *set* goals, but to live purposefully, serve generously, and trust that joy will meet you in the work itself.

Expert Voices

John C. Norcross, PhD, behavioral change researcher, University of Scranton, on the gap between intentions and outcomes. (Inc.com)

Ariana M. Chao, PhD, Yale Stress Center, on cortisol's link to weight gain under stress. (PMC)

Jean Baptiste Bouillon Minois, MD, meta-analysis of ghrelin as a stress biomarker and appetite trigger. (PMC)

Judy Ho, PhD, Psychology Today columnist, on dopamine released by completing small, meaningful tasks. (Psychology Today)

# # #

Chapter 4

Think Critically

Critical thinking.
To think critically is not merely to ask questions; it is to step boldly into the unknown, to challenge the familiar, and to seek the Divine even in uncomfortable truths. It is to turn ideas upside down, to weigh them against each other, and most courageously, against our own cherished beliefs.

Some say that critical thinking is the birthright of the free soul. Yet, throughout history, those who have dared to live by this light have often paid a steep price. They have been imprisoned, tortured, thrown to lions, and even burned at the stake.

Why? Because nothing threatens the status quo more than an awakened mind. And yet I embrace this risk. This is my *raison d'être*, my reason for being. I choose the path of sacred inquiry, no matter the cost.

The great paradox is this: critical thinkers are rarely praised while they live. Whether they are right or wrong, their mere existence unsettles others. But truth is not a popularity contest. It is a calling. And for those of us who seek it, the journey is reward enough.

Let me share with you how this sacred practice of questioning has shaped my view of the world, and perhaps, help you cultivate your own flame of insight.

Gazing at the Heavens
Over 2,000 years ago, a Greek astronomer named Aristarchus of Samos dared to say that the Earth was not the center of the universe. He believed the sun occupied that place of honor. Imagine that, centuries before telescopes and satellites, he glimpsed the cosmic truth.

His contemporaries, however, including the mighty Aristotle and Ptolemy, rejected him. And yet, Aristarchus lived out his life, quietly faithful to the truth he had seen.

But when Galileo echoed these same ideas nearly two millennia later, the world had changed. The Church had become the guardian of doctrine, and Galileo's thoughts were not welcome. He was accused of heresy. He faced the Inquisition and was sentenced to house arrest for the remainder of his days.

Why? Because truth, especially spiritual truth that challenges earthly power has always been dangerous. And yet, it is in those crucibles that our light grows strongest.

In his 2020 book *Galileo and the Science Deniers*, astrophysicist Mario Livio suggests that this very moment marked the beginning of our modern struggle with science denial. I suspect that something even deeper was at play: the fear of losing control over the minds and hearts of the faithful.

A Parking Lot Revelation

Not long ago, I walked out of Lanterns Mall in Barbados and heard Christmas music floating on the breeze. It was early November. My first reaction was one of annoyance: *Already?* But then, something shifted in me.

I remembered the lights. How beautiful they are, these beacons in the dark. And suddenly, I felt grateful. Grateful for this season of light, of memory, of hope. But then the troublemaker in me, the critical thinker, came knocking. *Why do so many traditions celebrate light in the midst of winter?* I began to notice a pattern, a divine choreography perhaps.

- Hanuka, the Jewish festival of lights, commemorates the re-dedication of the Jewish Temple on Temple Mount in Jerusalem. Miraculously, a tiny amount of sacred oil kept the menorah burning for eight full days. It was believed that there was only enough oil for one day. This, too, is a December story.

- **Diwali**, celebrated by Hindus, Sikhs, and Jains, proclaims the triumph of light over darkness, knowledge over ignorance. It comes in late October or November, a celestial opening act for what is to come.

- **Christmas**, of course, marks the birth of the Light of the World. But what if it wasn't chosen at random? What if God, in His infinite wisdom, chose to send His Son to walk among us *precisely* in the midst of these global celebrations of light?

What if, hidden within our holidays, is a message written in sacred metaphor whispering across cultures: *Light is coming. Prepare your hearts.* Even the three wise men, who journeyed from afar bearing gifts might have been seekers drawn not just by a star, but by centuries of prophetic light? What if they had just celebrated their own Diwali and were inspired to follow that brightness to its divine source?

Divine Whispers in Everyday Rituals

Each morning and night, I play a quiet round of solitaire before rising or drifting off to sleep. It's more than a habit. It's a meditation. Sometimes, as I decide which card to move, I pause. I ask, not with words, but with the stillness of spirit, for guidance. And you know what? It always comes. Is it from God? Is it intuition? Is it my own soul speaking truths I've long forgotten?

Just may be there is some divine joy in playing games with me.

Occasionally, the answer turns out to be wrong. But even then, I don't lose faith. Because maybe the point isn't *accuracy*. maybe it's attunement. Maybe what matters is learning to listen.

Scientists today tell us we may be living in a super-sophisticated simulation, running on some divine quantum processor far beyond our comprehension. Perhaps. But even if that were true, it would still beg the ultimate question:

Who created the creators?
And so, I return to the beginning, not just of this chapter, but of life's sacred call: Think. Question. Wonder. And above all, *trust the light within you*.

Even when others turn away. Even when the questions outnumber the answers. Even when the truth costs more than comfort. Because that, dear reader, is the holy work of the critical thinker.

# # #

Chapter 5

Emergence
The Divine Pattern of Becoming

"In the beginning was the Word, and the Word was with God, and the
Word was God," John 1:1

Creation begins not with a clamor of competing forces, but with a single resonant Word, a pulse of pure intention from the heart of the Divine. From that primal utterance, all that has ever existed or will exist unfurls. Scientists call the birthplace of that unfurling a singularity; some jokingly call it a black hole, a point so condensed that heaven and earth were, indistinguishable, "without void," space and time nonexistent. Scripture and physics converge: before there was form, there was potential, unseen, unmeasurable, yet complete.

This is Strong Emergence: something utterly new arising from the Source, bearing no outward resemblance to the One from whom it emerges. Imagine the device in your hands, glass, metal, plastic, and silicon rearranged into a portal of global connection. The sand and wire in its veins have no concept of the video you are streaming, or the book you are reading, yet together they create an experience inconceivable to their individual grains. Likewise, atoms in your body know nothing of the dreams that quicken your heart, yet they allow you to love, to hope, to soar.

The Mathematics of The Mystery
Physicists estimate the universe to be about 13.8 billion years old. They do so not by guessing, but by listening to the language the Creator still speaks: mathematics. Cosmic background radiation, an echo of the first divine Word- tells the tale. Equations trace the cooling glow backward to that incandescent moment when "Let there be light" pierced the horizon of the singularity and flooded all of existence with radiance. Light was not the end but the beginning of ongoing creation.

Sub-atomic particles raced outward, cooling and gathering into hydrogen atoms, stars,galaxies, planets, and ultimately into you. Each breath you take, flavored by the scent of new mown grass, are remnants of those first photons. Each cell in your body is a museum of cosmic history. You are not merely a thirty-nine-year-old inhabitant of the twenty-first century; you are, in a very real sense, as old as the universe itself.

The Two Faces of Emergence
1. Strong Emergence, where the new whole defies prediction from its parts. Creation, consciousness, and even love belong here.
2. Weak Emergence, where the components remain recognizable even as they move in wondrous harmony. Think of a school of fish turning as one, or a flock of starlings weaving shapes across the evening sky.

Both forms whisper a common truth: connection amplifies possibility. When isolated elements meet, the meeting changes them, and us, in ways we could never foresee by studying the pieces alone.

You: A Living Remnant of the Word

If every particle within you was present in that primordial flash, then you carry the spark of the original Word.,"Let their be light." Scripture proclaims that humanity is made in God's image; physics affirms that we are sculpted from star-stuff. The convergence is astonishing: within your very being burns a sliver of the same creative fire that spoke galaxies into motion.

Gaze at your neighbor and you glimpse the Divine. Look in the mirror and you stand before sacred potential. Such knowledge demands a response:
• How will we treat one another if each face reflects God?
• How will we steward Earth if every river and mountain emerges from the same holy source?
• How courageously will we nurture our gifts, knowing they are echoes of the Creator's first gift?

A Call to Conscious Creation

Humanity now crafts emergences of its own, artificial intelligences, global networks, cures for ancient diseases. These wonders reveal our inheritance of creative power, yet they warn as well: the next great emergence could be our flourishing or our undoing. The choice is ours. Therefore, let us ground our actions in universal spiritual values: compassion, justice, humility, and reverence. Let every innovation honor life. Let every policy, every partnership, every personal decision resonate with the music of that first Word.

When we live this way, we participate in an ongoing Genesis. We become co-creators, aligning our small words with the great Logos that still reverberates through space and soul. We remember that we are one, not by preference or persuasion, but by origin.

A Benediction of Becoming
You are the breath of stars,
the echo of the primordial hymn,
the living poem of God's first Word.
May you rise each day in awe of your ancient light.
May you look upon every being, plant, animal, person, and say,
"I behold the Divine in you."
May your thoughts lift, your words heal, and your deeds kindle hope, so that what emerges from your life expands the circle of love.

Fellow travelers, the universe is still unfolding. Let us unfold with it, boldly, beautifully, together

# # #

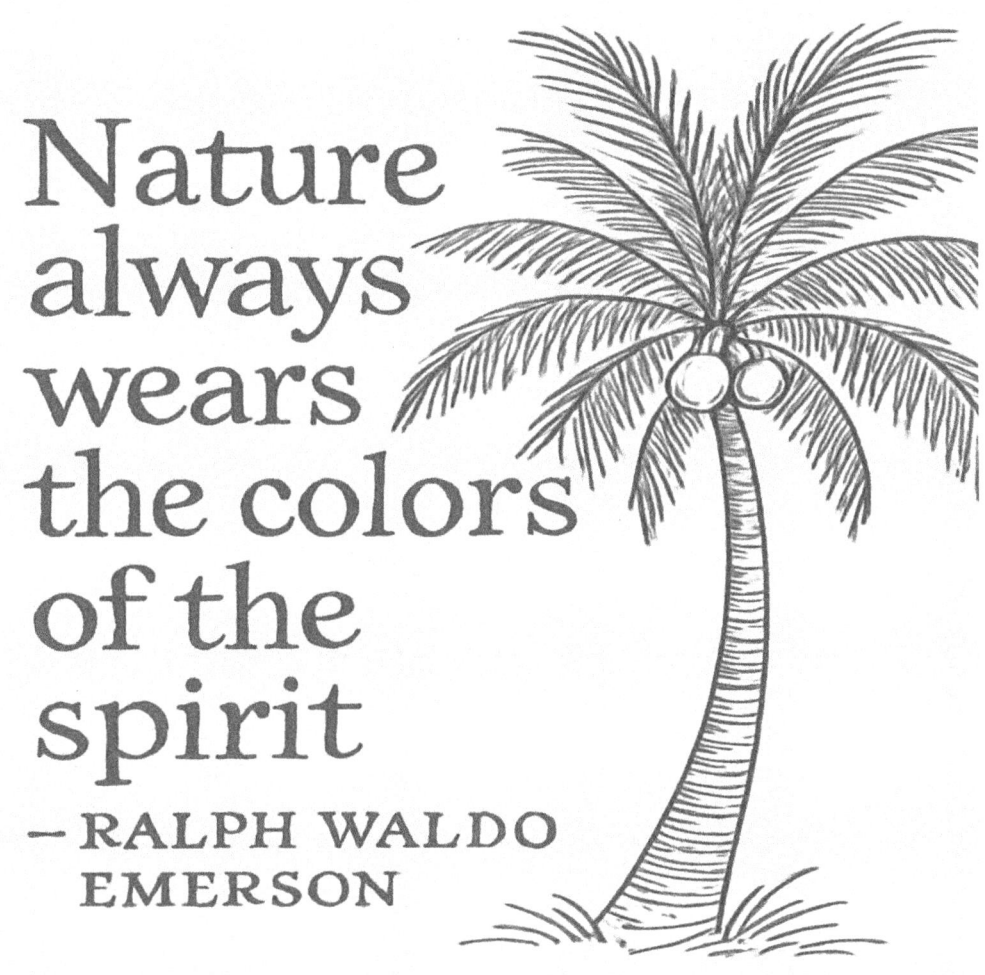

> Nature always wears the colors of the spirit
> — RALPH WALDO EMERSON

Chapter 6

The Gospel According to Green

A Living Palette

Step beneath the fronds of a coconut tree and you are bathed in green. Yet linger long enough, and the single hue dissolves into a thousand subtle shades, emerald and jade, sea-foam and sage. Try describing any one of them without using another color as a crutch, and you quickly discover a mystery: the "green" you experience is
born entirely inside your mind.

As neuroscientist David Eagleman observes, the world we see is less a direct download of reality and more "a constantly updated simulation," generated by the brain.[1]

The Symphony of Light

Every color begins as vibration. Photons cascading from the sun carry waves that dance between 540 and 580 terahertz, a silent hymn we later name green. When that light meets the coconut leaf, the leaf keeps what it needs for photosynthesis and reflects the rest. What bounces back is the slice of the spectrum our eyes can receive; the un-reflected bounty remains hidden, known only to the tree.

Isaac Newton's Opticks revealed that white light is a chorus of many colors, each with its own wavelength.[2] Three centuries later, Nobel laureates David Hubel and Torsten Wiesel showed that special cone cells in the retina translate those wavelengths into an electrical code, relaying them to the visual cortex at the back of the brain.[3] No light ever reaches that inner sanctuary; only pulses of current arrive. We "paint" the world behind closed doors of flesh and bone.

The Wonder of Diversity

Most of us carry three kinds of cones, red, green, and blue detectors, yet about one in four women possesses a rare fourth cone, enabling them to perceive millions of additional hues. Vision scientist Gabriele Jordan calls these observers "tetrachromats," living proof that the universe is far richer than any single set of eyes can grasp.[4]

Even the ordinary spectrum is not fixed. Some people with cross-wired senses, a condition known as synesthesia, literally hear color or taste sound. Neurologist Oliver Sacks chronicled patients who heard symphonies in sunsets, reminding us that the borders of perception are porous.[5]

Forging a Common Language
How, then, do we ever agree on what is "green"? From infancy, society hands us a shared dictionary. A mother points to a houseplant and says, "green"; eventually, the child marries that word to her private sensation. The agreement is profound, allowing us to cooperate, avoid danger, and build civilizations, yet it is also limiting. Conformity can blind us to fresh insight.

Copernicus dared to look at the sky and declare that Earth was not the center of everything. In 1956, Samuel Shelton founded the International Flat Earth Society in stubborn protest of centuries of astronomical evidence.

History swings between these poles: courageous visionaries who expand the map, and fearful gatekeepers who cling to yesterday's borders.

An Invitation to Holy Curiosity
Spiritually, the lesson is plain. Scripture tells us that "we walk by faith, not by sight" (2 Cor 5:7). If even color is a constructed story, how much more might our other certainties be provisional? The Apostle Paul urged believers to "be transformed by the renewing of your mind" (Rom 12:2). Renewing begins when we question the stories we inherited and open ourselves to God's ever-unfolding revelation in creation.

Let the coconut tree become your teacher:
Observe deeply. Notice nuance, the quiet transition between lime and forest green.
Question boldly. Ask what lies beyond your present level of understanding.
Trust humbly. Recognize that your vision, however vivid, is partial and incomplete.
Divine reality exceeds any single viewpoint.

From Shade to Light
When we embrace the hidden vastness behind every leaf, our hearts enlarge, and our minds expand. We honor the Creator who "makes everything beautiful in its time" (Eccl 3:11) and we honor one another, knowing each person may see a color we cannot yet imagine.

Fellow seekers of truth: may we leave this chapter resolved to look again, at the world, at each other, and at ourselves with sanctified wonder. For somewhere in those unnoticed frequencies of grace lies the next breakthrough that will heal, unite, and inspire us all.

References

1. Eagleman, D. Incognito: The Secret Lives of the Brain. (2011).

2. Newton, I. Opticks. (1704).

3. Hubel, D. H., & Wiesel, T. N. "Receptive fields of single neurons in the cat's striate cortex," Journal of Physiology (1959).

4. Jordan, G., et al. "Anomalous trichromatism and tetrachromatism," Vision Research (2010).

5. Sacks, O. Musicophilia. (2007).

# # #

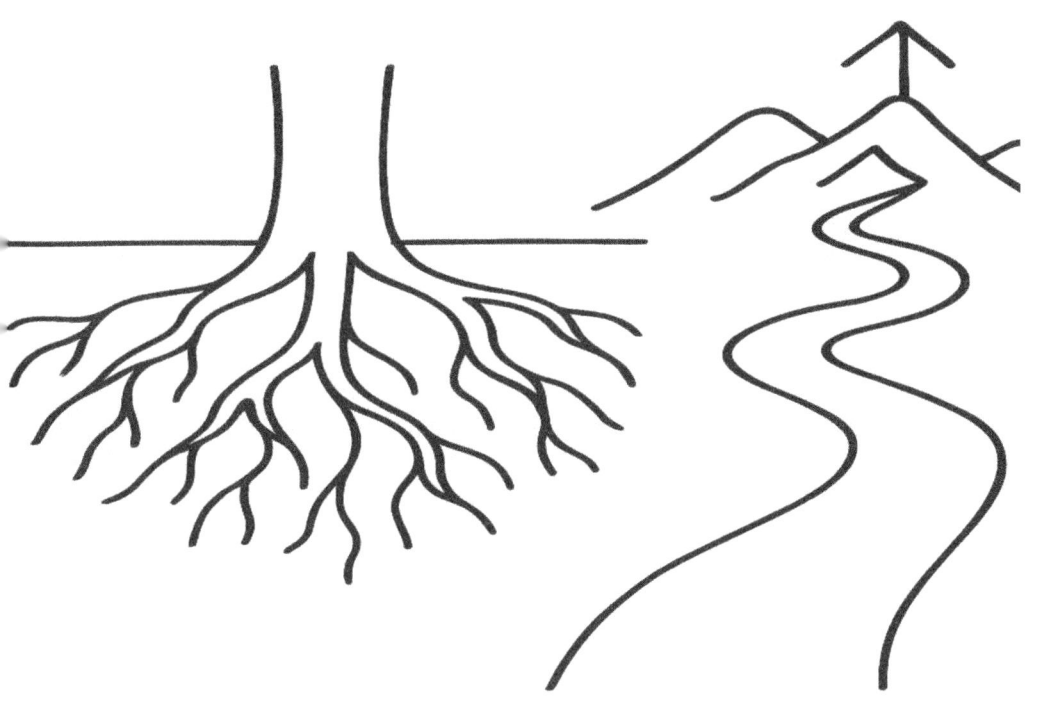

Chapter 7

Making History Relevant

> **"If you know from whence you came,
> There is no limit to where you can go."**
> *James Baldwin*

It was a warm Caribbean evening when I found myself seated among scholars at The University of the West Indies, Cave Hill Campus. The lecture that day focused on a pressing question: How do we make history relevant again?

A quiet but clear concern echoed throughout the room; history, once a pillar of education, was now seen as fading in importance. One professor lamented, "My classes have shrunk so much I now hold lectures in my office." His voice held both frustration and a quiet sense of defeat.

As I listened, I could not help but reflect. I've come to believe that in the West Indies, and in many parts of the world, we too often neglect to view education, especially history, from the perspective of the student. We focus on content, not connection. But to teach history effectively, we must *ignite the soul*, not just deliver the syllabus.

That evening something awakened within me, a familiar stirring of what I lovingly call my "inborn troublemaker instinct." It was time to speak up. And not for the sake of argument, but for the sake of a generation being left behind by the very stories that could liberate them.

A Lesson from the Sky
Years ago in Miami, I was mentoring a group of young people from underprivileged neighborhoods. They struggled in school, and many had already resigned themselves to a future of limited opportunities.

At the time, I served as a Flight Instructor with the U.S. Air Force Auxiliary. Through our youth aviation program, we took cadets on practice search-and-rescue missions. While they couldn't yet fly solo or act as pilots-in-command, they were allowed to join as observers. And how they loved it, being around aircraft, feeling the rumble of the engines, imagining the skies as their future.

But we had a rule: to remain on *flight status*, you had to maintain a **B+ average** in school. That became the barrier for some.

Not because they lacked ability, but because they lacked belief in themselves, and in what they came from.

I knew then that our greatest mission wasn't in the sky. It was down on earth in the heart and mind of each young person.

Reclaiming Their Roots

To change their mindset, I began by teaching them a lesson in genetics and resilience. Traits passed from generation to generation, physical, mental, emotional filtered through hardship and honed through struggle. What remains is strength refined by fire.

In 1619, the first enslaved Africans arrived in Virginia aboard *The White Lion*, a ship that marked the beginning of centuries of dehumanizing bondage. But before they even reached the Americas, these people endured an unimaginable trial: captured from the strongest stock, forced to march for hundreds of miles in shackles, through jungle, desert, and disease, many perishing along the way.

Those who survived, those who made it to the coast, faced the horrors of the Middle Passage, packed below deck like cargo, lying shoulder to shoulder on pallettes 18" wide, and in darkness for months. Little food. No sanitation. Suffering became a silent companion.

And yet, they survived.

Once in the New World, they faced over 400 years of systemic cruelty, including laws that *explicitly forbade their education* (Acts of the Southern Colonies, 18th century). They were denied the right to read, write, and dignity. But not intelligence. Not faith. Not hope.

That blood runs in your veins, I told my students. You are the descendants of the strongest, smartest, most resilient people to ever walk this earth. Your very existence is a miracle of survival. And I looked them in the eyes and said:
"With the spirit of your ancestors alive in you, a B+ should not even make you sweat."

Transforming Identity Through History

When a young person sees their heritage not as shame, but as triumph, something profound happens. Their expectations rise. Their self-worth awakens. Teachers begin to respond differently. Parents breathe easier. Possibility replaces despair.

From there, they become unstoppable,

whether as a President, scientist, artist, pilot, professor, athlete, or world-changer.

They stop asking, *"Can I?"* and start declaring, *"Watch me."*

A Spiritual Reclamation
Scripture reminds us:

> "You will know them by their fruits."
> *Matthew 7:16*

And the fruit of this historical reclamation is rich. When we teach history not merely as a list of events, but as a mirror of endurance, we give our youth back their divine inheritance.

History is not dead. It is alive in us. It is the compass pointing us toward our God-given purpose.

To every educator, parent, and mentor: make history relevant. Make it personal. Make it sacred.

Only then will our youth take flight and never look down again.

References & Suggested Reading:

- Baldwin, James. *The Fire Next Time*. Vintage, 1963.
- Alexander, Michelle. *The New Jim Crow*. The New Press, 2010.
- Equiano, Olaudah. *The Interesting Narrative of the Life of Olaudah Equiano*. 1789.
- Berlin, Ira. *Many Thousands Gone: The First Two Centuries of Slavery in North America*. Harvard University Press, 1998.
- Davis, David Brion. *Inhuman Bondage*. Oxford University Press, 2006.

# # #

Chapter 8

Souls in Passage:

The Journey of Indentured Servants: and Lessons They Left Behind

Between 1619 and 1865, a tide of humanity flowed across the Atlantic. They came chasing a dream. They came in chains. All came bearing burdens. All came with a spark of divine hope. Indentured servants and convicts were among the first laborers in the American colonies. Their paths were hard. Their faith, endurance, and transformation inspire us.

The Spirit of Indenture

Indentured servants were often young, poor, and desperate. Despite their limitations, they made a courageous exchange: a contract of service for a chance at something greater.

As Dr. David W. Galenson of the University of Chicago, a leading scholar of early American labor, noted, *"Indentured servitude was the institutional response to a critical labor shortage... and it was a pathway through which poor Europeans could reinvent themselves in the New World[1].

Despite grueling conditions, filthy ships, malnutrition, and disease, these travelers pressed on. Their story mirrors the pilgrim's journey: each step forward taken on faith. These individuals remind us that God does not need us to be perfect to begin again, only willing.

Harvesting with Hope
When they arrived, indentured servants were set to work on plantations, farms, and in homes. Historian Edmund S. Morgan wrote in *American Slavery, American Freedom* that "the early American dream was written in sweat."[2] These servants quite literally cultivated the soil from which the United States would rise.

Some, after years of backbreaking labor, received land and became freemen. Others, though broken by hardship, passed on the seeds of resilience to future generations. Their struggle speaks to the spiritual truth found in Galatians 6:9: *"Let us not grow weary in doing good, for at the proper time we will reap a harvest if we do not give up."*

From Chains to Change: The Convict's Journey

Alongside indentured servants came another group, criminals exiled by the British justice system. Historian Roger Ekirch, in *Bound for America*, writes that nearly 50,000 convicts were transported to America in the 18th century, often for petty crimes like theft[3].

Though stigmatized, many of these individuals found second chances in the New World. They worked, worshiped, and in time, some found redemption. Their stories prove what Scripture has long taught: *"Where sin increased, grace increased all the more"* (Romans 5:20). Even those cast away by men may be called home by God.

The Turning Tide

As the 18th century ended, slavery began to replace both indentured servitude and convict labor. Historian Ira Berlin described this shift as, "part of a larger tragedy:" "The rise of slavery was not just a story of labor demand, it was a story of human devaluation."[4] What was once a system of temporary hardship became, tragically, one of perpetual bondage.

Still, the era of indenture and convict labor offers a sacred lesson. These individuals were more than laborers. The early immigrants to the Americas were mostly the undesirables of Europe. One has to wonder how their DNA and lived experience inform our societies during slavery and beyond. They were also vessels of courage, transformation, and divine potential. Their lives prove that greatness often begins in places others overlook.

As the Americas moved away from immigrants who were undesirable in their home countries, the need for groups that could be looked down on and discriminated against subsided. We saw the end of Slavery and the beginning of a move towards ethnic and sexual equality.

Legacy and Reflection
We are all, in some way, spiritual indentured servants. We sign on for difficult tasks in life, sometimes unknowingly, and we labor through suffering, only to discover that each trial refines us. As author and theologian Henri Nouwen reminds us, "The spiritual life is not a life before, after, or beyond our everyday existence. No, the spiritual life can only be real when it is lived in the midst of the pains

and joys of the here and now."[5]

Let us remember the souls who crossed oceans and endured injustice. Not as statistics. Not as shadows of the past. But as lights, flickering, fragile, yet enduring.

Their journeys teach us:

- That hardship can purify.
- That grace is found even in exile.
- That freedom, true freedom, begins in the heart.

May we walk with courage, as they did, toward a future we cannot yet see but are divinely called to build.

References
1. Galenson, David W. *White Servitude in Colonial America: An Economic Analysis*. Cambridge University Press, 1981.
2. Morgan, Edmund S. *American Slavery, American Freedom: The Ordeal of Colonial Virginia*. W.W. Norton & Company, 1975.
3. Ekirch, A. Roger. *Bound for America: The Transportation of British Convicts to the Colonies, 1718–1775*. Oxford University Press, 1987.
4. Berlin, Ira. *Many Thousands Gone: The First Two Centuries of Slavery in North America*. Harvard University Press, 1998.
5. Nouwen, Henri J.M. *The Spiritual Life: Eight Essential Titles*. Harper One, 2011.

# # #

Chapter 9

Rock-Cut Tombs

A Reflection on Faith, History, and Transformation

Learning is the sacred process of connecting the old with the new, a divine unfolding of wisdom. When we link familiar truths with fresh insight, we deepen our understanding and illuminate the path ahead. I invite you to view even the most ancient traditions with new eyes, for it is through questioning and re-examining what we believe that true learning and spiritual growth emerge.

Consider the rock-cut tomb, a resting place hewn from solid stone or carved from caves in hilly terrains. These tombs were once reserved for the wealthy, who could afford the land and labor to chisel eternity into the earth. In ancient Israel, the body of the deceased was washed, wrapped in linen, and respectfully placed in these sacred chambers before sunset, especially during holy seasons like Passover.

Christ Himself, crucified just before this sacred festival, was hurriedly entombed to avoid ritual impurity, which would have required cleansing in a Mikveh, a ritual bath still preserved here in Barbados, at our historic synagogue.

The tombs were sealed not only to guard against decay and animals but also to honor the dignity of the dead. Once decomposition was complete, bones were collected and placed into ossuaries, beautifully adorned boxes or vaults meant for secondary burial. This practice, which dates back to 3000 BCE, vanished for nearly a millennium before reappearing in Jerusalem around 900 BCE. As described in *A Global History of Architecture* by Ching and Jarzombek, the tradition spans civilizations, from the Midas Monument in ancient Turkey (1450 BCE) to Petra in Jordan (100 CE).

In Jewish and Islamic custom, embalming is forbidden, as it is seen as desecrating the body. Instead, the body is placed intact in the tomb and left to return to dust, a sacred echo of Genesis 3:19: "For dust you are, and to dust you shall return." Rock-cut tombs, especially in Jerusalem, are costly and constructed with the understanding that they are to be reused, designed for impermanence, yet holding eternal meaning.

There are three deeply symbolic sites in Israel connected to the burial of Christ. The first, the Church of the Holy Sepulcher, consecrated in

335 CE, rests on the Via Dolorosa, the path of Jesus' final walk. The second, known as the Garden Tomb, is a serene place carved into a hillside called Skull Hill. Owned by The Garden Tomb Association of the UK, it offers a compelling alternative for Protestant visitors. The third, in the town of Talpiot, is where archaeologists uncovered ossuaries in a family tomb, including inscriptions like "Yeshua bar Yosef" (Jesus, son of Joseph), "Miriam" (Mary), and "Yose" (Joseph), a name listed in Mark 6:3 as one of Jesus' brothers. Another ossuary bore the inscription "Yehuda bar Yeshua", possibly "Judah, son of Jesus," as described by Simcha Jacobovici and Charles Pellegrino in *The Jesus Family Tomb*.

Jesus, an itinerant preacher, could not afford a tomb. His burial site was generously provided by Joseph of Arimathea, a wealthy follower. If the resurrection were only spiritual, the ossuary of Christ might exist somewhere. But belief in a physical resurrection, shared by Sunni Muslims, rejects that possibility altogether. Faiths may diverge in theology, yet they all yearn for transcendence.

The Shroud of Turin, or *Sacra Sindone*, surfaced in 1354, bearing what many claim is the image of Christ. But the canonical Gospels describe Jesus' burial wrappings as torn strips, raising questions about the shroud's authenticity. Whether one believes in the ossuaries, the shroud, or the tombs themselves, the spiritual truth remains: these stories invite us to explore, to question, to deepen our journey with reverence.

I do not ask that you accept these claims without inquiry. In fact, I rejoice if this chapter stirs debate, reflection, or a research quest of your own. For if even one reader is inspired to ask deeper questions or examine long-held beliefs, I'll join the chorus and sing with joy: *Oh Happy Day!*

References

Ching, F., Jarzombek, M., & Prakash, V. (2010). *A Global History of Architecture*. Wiley.

Jacobovici, S., & Pellegrino, C. (2007). *The Jesus Family Tomb: The Discovery, the Investigation, and the Evidence That Could Change History*. HarperOne.

The Bible. Genesis 3:19; Mark 6:3.

The Garden Tomb Association. https://gardentomb.com

Church of the Holy Sepulchre. Encyclopedia Britannica.

Shroud of Turin Research Project. https://shroud.com

# # #

Chapter 10

Leadership is not a title; it is a **calling** that whispers to every soul.[1] Whether you are the designated head, the newest recruit, or the senior sage, the spark of leadership lies within you, waiting to be ignited by purpose, vision, and love.

Who Is a Leader?

As strategist Tony Robbins observes, "Every person has the capacity to lead from exactly where they stand."[2]

- The formal leader
- The junior teammate
- The veteran voice of experience
- The quiet observer who sees what others miss

All can step forward when the moment arrives. Leadership is everyone's sacred potential.

Why Do We Lead?

We reject the counterfeit motive of controlling others. Leadership is not about bending people to our will. True, spirit-filled leadership exists to:

1. Accomplish what no single person could achieve alone.[3]
2. Bless stakeholders, those we serve, not just ourselves.[4]
3. Multiply leaders. Every great leader lights new candles until the room shines.

Leading the Self First

"So then, by their fruit you will recognize them.", Matthew 7:20 (NIV)[5]

Before shepherding others, a leader must shepherd themselves:

- Master emotions under pressure.
- Walk in integrity when unseen.
- Remain humble in success and courageous in loss.

Leadership begins in the hidden places of the heart; only then can public influence bear good fruit.

How Do Great Leaders Lead?

1. By Example. *"Leadership is influence, nothing more, nothing less.",* John C. Maxwell[6]
2. By Vision. *"People don't buy what you*

do; they buy why you do it.",
Simon Sinek[7]

3. By Empowering Others. *"The growth and well-being of people is the highest goal of the servant-leader."*, Robert K. Greenleaf[8]

4. By Encouraging Excellence, Not Commanding Compliance. *"Great leaders do not command from above, they lift from beside."*[9]

In volunteer organizations, thunder without love soon turns to silence. The most gifted members leave first, and with them goes the organization's soul. Influence built on inspiration endures; influence built on intimidation collapses.

Practice: The Path to Mastery
Leadership is forged, not born. We practice by:

- Listening when it is easier to speak
- Admitting fault when pride begs for defense
- Choosing the high road when retaliation tempts us

- Celebrating others' victories as if they were our own

As Jim Collins found in his study of enduring companies, *"Level 5 leaders channel their ego needs away from themselves and toward the larger goal."*[10]

Lead with Love
Leadership, at its highest, is service, drawing out the divine in others, fanning dormant embers into blazing purpose. We are not here to rule; we are here to reveal.

> "Let your light shine before others, that they may see your good deeds and glorify your Father in heaven." , Matthew 5:16 (NIV)[5]

Let your legacy be measured not by the number of followers you amassed, but by the number of **new lights** you helped to shine.

May these insights guide you to lead yourself first, ignite the spark in others, and walk the path of servant-leadership, where every step is an act of love and every victory a chorus of shared light.

1. **Footnotes**
   Ruth B. Nash, *Leadership as Calling*, Journal of Spiritual Leadership, 2019.
2. Tony Robbins, *Unlimited Power*, Simon & Schuster, 1986.
3. Peter G. Northouse, *Leadership: Theory and Practice*, Sage, 2022.
4. Max De Pree, *Leadership Is an Art*, Doubleday, 1989.
5. The Holy Bible, New International Version.
6. John C. Maxwell, *Developing the Leader Within You 2.0*, Harper Collins, 2018.
7. Simon Sinek, *Start With Why*, Portfolio, 2009.
8. Robert K. Greenleaf, *Servant Leadership*, Paulist Press, 1977.
9. Adapted teaching widely attributed to leadership trainer Leslie Parrott (paraphrased).
10. Jim Collins, *Good to Great*, Harper Business, 2001.

Reference List

- Collins, Jim. *Good to Great: Why Some Companies Make the Leap… and Others Don't*. HarperBusiness, 2001.
- De Pree, Max. *Leadership Is an Art*. Doubleday, 1989.
- Greenleaf, Robert K. *Servant Leadership: A Journey into the Nature of Legitimate Power and Greatness*. Paulist Press, 1977.
- Holy Bible, New International Version. Biblica, 2011.
- Maxwell, John C. *Developing the Leader Within You 2.0*. HarperCollins, 2018.
- Nash, Ruth B. "Leadership as Calling." *Journal of Spiritual Leadership*, vol. 4, no. 2, 2019, pp. 15–27.
- Northouse, Peter G. *Leadership: Theory and Practice*. 10th ed., Sage, 2022.
- Robbins, Tony. *Unlimited Power: The New Science of Personal Achievement*. Simon & Schuster, 1986.
- Sinek, Simon. *Start With Why: How Great Leaders Inspire Everyone to Take Action*. Portfolio, 2009.
- Parrott, Leslie. *The Art of Relational Leadership*. Zondervan, 2010.

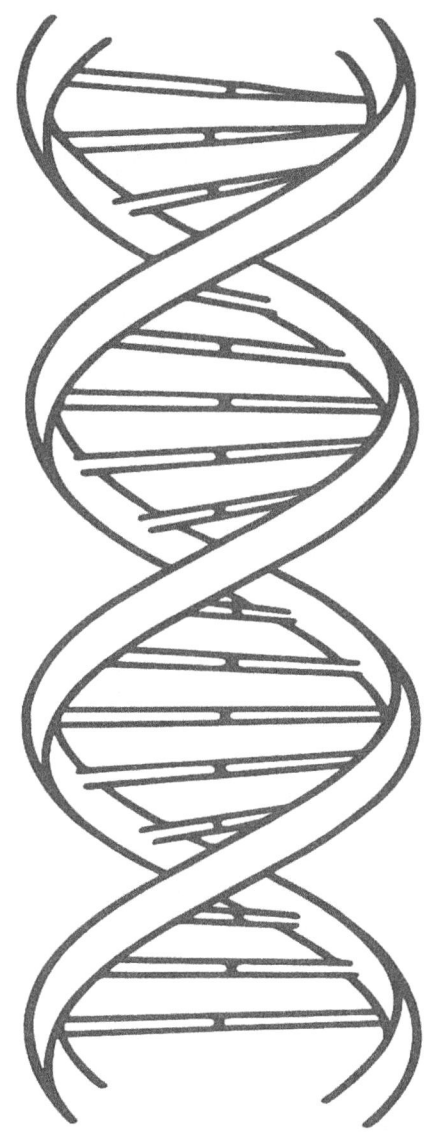

Chapter 11

The Code of Creation

In the vast, intricate dance of existence, there is a divine signature woven into the heart of all living things, a silent code, written in a language beyond words, yet pulsing with life. We call it DNA: *Deoxyribonucleic Acid*. To the scientist, it is a molecule. To the seeker, it is sacred scripture encoded in the body. And to those of us who dare to blend science with spirit, it is nothing less than the programming language of God.

The Divine Architecture of Life
DNA is no ordinary structure. It is a polymer, a chemical composition made of countless molecules bonded in elegant harmony. It exists not in chaos, but in astonishing order. These threads are organized into chromosomes, forming the backbone of every known living organism on Earth, even viruses owe their existence to its design.

What makes DNA remarkable is not only its composition but its intelligence. It is *heuristic*, which means it learns, adapts, and evolves. This divine software does not merely store data, it interprets, corrects, and sometimes even repairs itself. It is double-stranded, forming the now-famous double helix, a celestial spiral echoing the galaxies in space and the kundalini in the spine.

Each strand is a **mirror** of the other, not in identical repetition, but in *reverse order*, like the yin and the yang, complementing and correcting one another. Within this helix is embedded an error correction system, a backup mechanism, and layers of redundancy that testify to the precision of its Creator.

The Sacred Ratio: 98 to 2

We often marvel that only 2% of DNA contains the instructions necessary for life's biological functions genes that direct our growth, healing, and metabolism. The other 98%? Scientists once called it "junk," unable to interpret its purpose. But we now understand that it holds descriptive information, the blueprint for our physical characteristics, tendencies, and predispositions. It is the poetry of our being, not just the commands.

Does that not reflect our own lives? A small part of what we *do* maybe measurable, but the larger part, who we *are,* remains mysterious, beautiful, and sacred.

The Divine Programmer

Modern software engineers recognize something extraordinary: DNA behaves like a programming language, only far more advanced than anything we have written. Every strand, every sequence, every base pair reflects intentional design.

Like human programmers, God leaves fingerprints in the code. One such fingerprint is known in computer science as **KLOC,** *thousands of lines of code*, used to estimate the number of likely errors. Each programmer has a unique KLOC signature. Usually the error rate for an experienced programmer is 10 errors per KLOC. Some programs are more complex, some require more testing. But no program is flawless.

If DNA is the programming language of God, then we are not accidents, we are living lines of divine code, constantly being interpreted by the cosmos itself. We have not been able to determine God's KLOC because the code is self correcting, the program is so large, and many of the codes can alter the code of other organisms

Are We in a Simulation?

This awe-inspiring complexity has led some philosophers and scientists to wonder: Are we real? Or are we part of a grand simulation?

Thinkers like Nick Bostrom (of Yale and Oxford) and David Chalmers (NYU) have explored what's now called the Simulation Hypothesis. It presents three possibilities:

There's a significant chance, perhaps 50%, that all of reality is a simulation.

Everything we know, including our thoughts and memories, could be simulated.

Or perhaps only *you* are real, and everyone else is part of the simulation.

It may sound strange, even unsettling. But perhaps it's another way of saying what mystics have always taught: that reality is not as fixed as we believe, and that we are part of something far more wondrous than the physical senses alone can perceive.

The Test of Consciousness

How, then, do we know what is real? In computer science, there's a concept known as the Turing Test, a way to determine whether an artificial intelligence can convincingly mimic human behavior.

But spiritual tradition gives us another test, perhaps more important: Are we conscious? Are we aware of the divine within us?

If the answer is yes, if we can reflect, choose love, embrace truth, then regardless of the architecture of our reality, we are fulfilling a higher purpose.

And what is that purpose? To awaken. To remember who we are. To honor the divine code within ourselves and others.

The Christ Within the Code

In the Gospel of John, it is written: "In the beginning was the Word, and the Word was with God, and the Word was God." The "Word" here can be understood as logos, divine logic, divine reason, divine code.

The Christ is not only a historical figure, but a living pattern, a code of compassion, forgiveness, and divine love written into the spiritual DNA of humanity. To follow the path of Christ is to activate that higher code to become not merely a copy of divine intent, but a co-creator with the Creator.

You are more than flesh and blood.
You are code and consciousness.
You are biology and spirit.
You are the living program of a loving God.

And the next time you feel small or insignificant, remember:
Even your cells are singing hymns in the language of heaven.

# # #

Final Reflection

The final proof of any spiritual insight is not what it makes you *believe*, but what it makes you *become*.

So I leave you with one last question:

What would change in your life, today, if you truly believed the Divine is present in the ordinary, and that you were placed here to build something that love will recognize?

Don't answer it quickly.

Answer it with your life.

www.ingramcontent.com/pod-product-compliance
Lightning Source LLC
Chambersburg PA
CBHW040231110526
44582CB00001B/21